MW01292382

War Room
Prayer Journal

*"Write the vision, and make
it plain…" Habakkuk 2:2*

This Journal belongs to:

....

Spirit Life Publications

"Verily, verily, I say unto you, Whatsoever ye shall ask the Father in my name, he will give it you. Hitherto have ye asked nothing in my name: ask, and ye shall receive, that your joy may be full. These things have I spoken unto you in proverbs: but the time cometh, when I shall no more speak unto you in proverbs, but I shall shew you plainly of the Father. At that day ye shall ask in my name: and I say not unto you, that I will pray the Father for you: For the Father himself loveth you, because ye have loved me, and have believed that I came out from God."
John 16:23-27

Call
TO ME
and i will
AnSWeR
you
and will tell you
Great & Hidden
THINGS
THAT YOU
HAVE NOT KNOWN
Jeremiah 33.3

"No erudition, no purity of diction, no width of mental outlook, no flowers of eloquence, no grace of person atone for lack of fire. Prayer ascends by fire. Flame gives prayer access as well as wings, acceptance as well as energy. There is no incense without fire; no prayer without flame." - E. M. Bounds

"Bear up the hands that hang down, by faith and prayer; support the tottering knees. Have you any days of fasting and prayer? Storm the throne of grace and persevere therein, and mercy will come down." - John Wesley

"Bear up the hands that hang down, by faith and prayer; support the tottering knees. Have you any days of fasting and prayer? Storm the throne of grace and persevere therein, and mercy will come down." - John Wesley

"Before the great revival in Gallneukirchen broke out, Martin Boos spent hours and days and often nights in lonely agonies of intercession. Afterwards, when he preached, his words were as flame, and the hearts of the people as grass." - D.M. McIntyre. D.D.

"Oh, for closest communion with God, till soul and body, head, face, and heart shine with Divine brilliancy! But oh! for a holy ignorance of our shining!" - Robert Murray M'Cheyne

"Depend upon it, if you are bent on prayer, the devil will not leave you alone. He will molest you, tantalize you, block you, and will surely find some hindrances, big or little or both. And we sometimes fail because we are ignorant of his devices. I do not think he minds our praying about things if we leave it at that. What he minds, and opposes steadily, is the prayer that prays on until it is prayed through, assured of the answer".
- Mary Warburton Booth

"Do not have your concert first, and then tune your instrument afterwards. Begin the day with the Word of God and prayer, and get first of all into harmony with Him." - James Hudson Taylor

LOVE HOPES all things

1 Cor. 13.7

"Our sufficiency is of God. Difficulties melt in His presence. In Him are those mighty, overcoming energies, which accomplish the possible and the impossible with equal readiness. The real resources are with Him for the evangelizing and the redeeming of the world. But He has not been able to do many mighty works in the non-Christian lands, because of our unbelief as a Church. We have not possessed our possessions. God has been waiting to be honored by the faith of a generation that would call upon Him for really large outpourings of His power." J. Lovell Murray(SVM)

"Ah, prayer turns trembling saints into great victors! There is no such thing as surrender, or even discouragement, to a man who dwells in the secret place of the Most High and abides under the shadow of the Almighty." - Henry W. Frost

"I have seen many men work without praying, though I have never seen any good come out of it; but I have never seen a man pray without working." - James Hudson Taylor

"The men that will change the colleges and seminaries here represented are the men that will spend the most time alone with God. It takes time for the fires to burn. It takes time for God to draw near and for us to know that He is there. It takes time to assimilate His truth. You ask me, How much time? I do not know. I know it means time enough to forget time." - John R. Mott

"Oh! men and brethren, what would this heart feel if I could but believe that there were some among you who would go home and pray for a revival men whose faith is large enough, and their love fiery enough to lead them from this moment to exercise unceasing intercessions that God would appear among us and do wondrous things here, as in the times of former generations." -C. H. Spurgeon

"We Christians too often substitute prayer for playing the game. Prayer is good; but when used as a substitute for obedience, it is nothing but a blatant hypocrisy, a despicable Pharisaism...To your knees, man! and to your Bible! Decide at once! Don't hedge! Time flies! Cease your insults to God, quit consulting flesh and blood. Stop your lame, lying, and cowardly excuses. Enlist!" - C. T. Studd

"The reason why many fail in battle is because they wait until the hour of battle. The reason why others succeed is because they have gained their victory on their knees long before the battle came...Anticipate your battles; fight them on your knees before temptation comes, and you will always have victory." - R. A. Torrey

"A sermon in shoes is often more eloquent than a sermon on paper." - Theodore L. Cuyler

"To arouse one man or woman to the tremendous power of prayer for others, is worth more than the combined activity of a score of average Christians." - A. J. Gordon

"I would rather train twenty men to pray, than a thousand to preach; - A minister's highest mission ought to be to teach his people to pray." -H. MacGregor

"Are you living for the things you are praying for?" - Austin Phelps

"A prayerless man is proud and independent, and any church that neglects corporate prayer is sadly no better. Only God's humble and needy children take the time to pray. Everyone else is just going through the motions and naively trusting in their own strength!" - David Smithers

"We need a baptism of clear seeing. We desperately need seers who can see through the mist--Christian leaders with prophetic vision. Unless they come soon it will be too late for this generation. And if they do come we will no doubt crucify a few of them in the name of our worldly orthodoxy." -A. W. Tozer

WHERE your TREASURE is there your HEART will be also

MATTHEW 6.21

"The time factor in prayer is very important. In the exercise of prayer God is not tied to our clocks. Neither is He at the other end of the phone to receive and answer our two-minute calls. It takes time to know the mind of God, to shut out the material things of earth and to be wholly abandoned." -Hugh C. C. McCullough

"He can do all things who prays well. All soul-winners have conquered on their knees. Wherever the secret of prevailing prayer is found, something supernatural will come to pass." - G. F. Oliver

"No system of doctrine, preaching and worship which fails to develop prayer, faith, spiritual labor, and success in converting souls from sin, can long have the face to claim to be the religion of Jesus Christ!" -William W. Patton

"We must continue in prayer if we are to get an outpouring of the Spirit. Christ says there are some things we shall not get, unless we pray and fast, yes, "prayer and fasting." We must control the flesh and abstain from whatever hinders direct fellowship with God." - Andrew Bonar

Date:

"The history of missions is the history of answered prayer. From Pentecost to the Haystack meeting in New England and from the days when Robert Morrison landed in China to the martyrdom of John and Betty Stam, prayer has been the source of power and the secret of spiritual triumph." -Samuel Zwemer

"This much is sure in all churches, forgetting party labels; the smallest meeting numerically is the prayer- meeting. If weak in prayer we are weak everywhere." - Leonard Ravenhill

"How long will it take us to learn that our shortest route to the man next door is by way of God's throne?" - A. T. Pierson

"Wherever the Church is aroused and the world's wickedness arrested, somebody has been praying." - A. T. Pierson

"How terrible is the cost of robbing God of time for prayer. When we rob God of time for quiet, we are robbing Him of ourselves. It is only in the quiet that we can really know Him and know ourselves, and be sure that we give ourselves back to Him. Oh, for God's sake, do not risk keeping the windows of Heaven closed by robbing God of time." (Keswick 1946) Gordon M. Guinness

"The missionary church is a praying church. The history of missions is a history of prayer. Everything vital to the success of the world's evangelization hinges on prayer. Are thousands of missionaries and tens of thousands of native workers needed? ÔPray ye therefore the Lord of the harvest, that He send forth laborers into His harvest." - John R. Mott

"God the Holy Ghost calls for crusaders. How many ministers would be in church if it were not their job? The answer will be found in the number who never go to the job that is outside." - Samuel Chadwick

I CAN DO
ALL THINGS
THROUGH HIM
WHO STRENGTHENS ME
PHILIPPIANS 4:13

"The evangelization of the world in this generation depends first of all upon a revival of prayer. Deeper than the need for men; deeper, far, than the need for money; aye, deep down at the bottom of our spiritless life is the need for the forgotten secret of prevailing, world-wide prayer." - Robert E. Speer

"Prayer alone will overcome the gigantic difficulties which confront the workers in every field." - John R. Mott

"The Church has not yet touched the fringe of the possibilities of intercessory prayer. Her largest victories will be witnessed when individual Christians everywhere come to recognize their priesthood unto God and day by day give themselves unto prayer." - John R. Mott

"If added power attends the united prayer of two or three, what mighty triumphs there will be when hundreds of thousands of consistent members of the Church are with one accord day by day making intercession for the extension of Christ's Kingdom." - John R. Mott

"The evangelization of the world in this generation depends first of all upon a revival of prayer. Deeper than the need for men; deeper, far, than the need for money; aye, deep down at the bottom of our spiritless life is the need for the forgotten secret of prevailing, world-wide prayer." - Robert E. Speer

"Faith and prayer are so inter-linked that faith is prayer and prayer is faith. You cannot separate them. You could not have the one without the other." - A. Lindsay Glegg

Date:

"I believe there is one thing for which God is very angry with our land, and for which His Holy Spirit is so little among us, and that is the neglect of united prayer; the appointed means of bringing down the Holy Spirit." - Brownlow North

"The neglect of prayer proves to my mind, that there is a large amount of practical infidelity. If the people believed that there was a real, existing, personal God, they would ask Him for what they wanted, and they would get what they asked. But they do not ask, because they do not believe or expect to receive." - Brownlow North

"Oh Christians, go more to the prayer-meetings." - Brownlow North

"From the day of Pentecost, there has been not one great spiritual awakening in any land which has not begun in a union of prayer, though only among two or three. And no such outward, upward movement has continued after such prayer meetings have declined. It is in exact proportion to the maintenance of such joint and believing supplication and intercession that the Word of the Lord in any land or locality has had free course and been glorified." - A. T. Pierson

"The disappearance of the 'prayer meeting' from the life of many churches is something which occasions widespread regret, even among many who would not normally attend." Indeed, the prayer meeting in which the laity participated freely is a legacy from the 1859 (Ulster) Revival...These prayer meetings were not in many cases in existence before the revival set in. The very establishment of them in the first instance, was an evidence that it was spring-time again in the Church of Christ, and the restoration of them today would be for her reviving once more." - John T. Carson

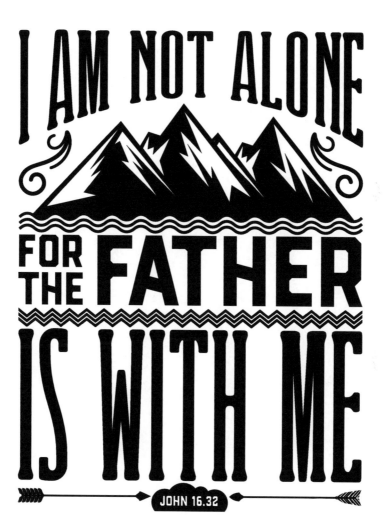

"All practical power over sin and over men depends on maintaining closet communion. Those who abide in the secret place with God show themselves mighty to conquer evil, and strong to work and to war for God. They are seers who read His secrets; they know His will; they are the meek whom He guides in judgment and teaches His way. They are His prophets who speak for Him to others, and even forecast things to come. They watch the signs of the times and discern His tokens and read His signals." - A. T. Pierson

"God has no greater controversy with His people today than this, that with boundless promises to believing prayer, there are so few who actually give themselves unto intercession." - A. T. Pierson

"You must pray with all your might. That does not mean saying your prayers, or sitting gazing about in church or chapel with eyes wide open while someone else says them for you. It means fervent, effectual, untiring wrestling with God...This kind of prayer be sure the devil and the world and your own indolent, unbelieving nature will oppose. They will pour water on this flame." - William Booth

"Preachers who never have revivals never weary of calling attention to everything objectionable in the methods of those who have powerful revivals...O ye fault-finders, beware lest when your Lord come, ye be found smiting your fellow servants, instead of working with them!" - B. T. Roberts

"Prayer is self-discipline. The effort to realize the presence and power of God stretches the sinews of the soul and hardens its muscles. To pray is to grow in grace. To tarry in the presence of the King leads to new loyalty and devotion on the part of the faithful subjects. Christian character grows in the secret-place of prayer. - Samuel M. Zwemer

"At Waterloo, the English troops obeying orders fell on their faces for a time and let the hot fire of the French artillery pass over them. Then they sprang to their feet and rushed to the thickest of the fight and beat back their foes. The Lord wants His people flat on their faces, before they attempt to meet the great crises of life." - A. T. Pierson

"A marble cutter, with chisel and hammer, was changing a stone into a statue. A preacher looking on said: 'I wish I could deal such changing blows on stony hearts. ' The workman answered: 'Maybe you could, if you worked like me, upon your knees.'"
- A. T. Pierson

"True prayer will achieve just as much as it costs us." - Samuel M. Zwemer

"The great battles, the battles that decide our destiny and the destiny of generations yet unborn, are not fought on public platforms, but in the lonely hours of the night and in moments of agony." - Samuel Logan Brengle

"The Word of God represents all the possibilities of God as at the disposal of true prayer." -A. T. Pierson

"What a man is on his knees before God in secret, that will he be before men: that much and no more." -Fred Mitchell

"Whether we like it or not, asking is the rule of the Kingdom. If you may have everything by asking in His Name, and nothing without asking, I beg you to see how absolutely vital prayer is." -C. H. Spurgeon

"Prayer - secret, fervent, believing prayer - lies at the root of all personal godliness." -
William Carey

"It is morally impossible to exercise trust in God while there is failure to wait upon Him for guidance and direction. The man who does not learn to wait upon the Lord and have his thoughts molded by Him will never possess that steady purpose and calm trust, which is essential to the exercise of wise influence upon others, in times of crisis and difficulty." - D. E. Hoste

"Should it not be recognized that the practice of prayer and intercession needs to be taught to young believers, or rather developed in young believers, quite as much, if not more so than other branches of the curriculum? Unless, however, we ourselves are, through constant persevering practice, truly alive unto God in this holy warfare, we shall be ineffective in influencing others. I am quite sure the rule holds that the more we pray the more we want to pray; the converse also being true." - D. E. Hoste

"Out of a very intimate acquaintance with D. L. Moody, I wish to testify that he was a far greater pray-er than he was preacher. Time and time again, he was confronted by obstacles that seemed insurmountable, but he always knew the way to overcome all difficulties. He knew the way to bring to pass anything that needed to be brought to pass. He knew and believed in the deepest depths of his soul that nothing was too hard for the Lord, and that prayer could do anything that God could do. " - R. A. Torrey.

"All great soul-winners have been men of much and mighty prayer, and all great revivals have been preceded and carried out by persevering, prevailing knee-work in the closet." - Samuel Logan Brengle

Date:

"God has created both the mother's milk and the child's desire to drink it. But the milk does not flow of itself into the child's mouth. No, the child must lie in its mother bosom and suck the milk diligently. God has created the spiritual food which we need. He has filled the soul of man with desire for this food, with an impulse to cry out for it and to drink it in. The spiritual milk, the nourishment of our souls, we receive through prayer. By means of fervent prayer we must receive it into our souls. As we do this we become stronger day by day, just like the infant at the breast." -
Sadhu Sundar Singh

YOU WILL RECEIVE POWER
W·H·E·N T·H·E
HOLY SPIRIT
HAS COME UPON YOU
AND YOU WILL
BE MY WITNESSES
ACTS 1.8

"We have found no means so much blessed to keep religion alive as FASTING and PRAYER." - Edward Payson

"The neglect of prayer is a grand hindrance to holiness." - John Wesley

"God will not let me get the blessing without asking. Today I am setting my face to fast and pray for enlightenment and refreshing. Until I can get up to the measure of at least two hours in pure prayer every day, I shall not be contented. Meditation and reading besides." - Andrew Bonar

"Beware in your prayers, above everything else, of limiting God, not only by unbelief, but by fancying that you know what He can do. Expect unexpected things, above all that we ask or think. Each time, before you Intercede, be quiet first, and worship God in His glory. Think of what He can do, and how He delights to hear the prayers of His redeemed people. Think of your place and privilege in Christ, and expect great things!" - Andrew Murray

"When we find anything promised in the Word of God, we are not to neglect to seek it because it is promised: but we are to pray for it on that very account. Thus saith the Lord God; I will yet for this be inquired of by the house of Israel, to do it for them; I will increase them with men like a flock" (Ezek. 36:37). The promise is absolute; but the time of its fulfillment depends upon the prayers of His people." - B. T. Roberts

"The reason why we obtain no more in prayer is because we expect no more. God usually answers us according to our own hearts." - Richard Allelne

"It is very much easier to work than to pray. Most of the missionaries are earnest workers. But are we all that we should be in the matter of prayer? Let us not suppose that just any sort of praying will do for China. We must all wrestle with God. I will not let Thee go unless Thou bless China. It must come to this if the conversion of the Chinese is ever to be an accomplished fact. Such is my conviction. Let me remind you that the greatest importunity is not incompatible with the profoundest submission to the Divine will." - Griffith John

"It must be remembered that there is spiritual wickedness at the back of all confusion and discord in the work of God. The servant of Christ must, therefore, practically recognize that his warfare is with these satanic beings and must be waged on his knees." - D. E. Hoste

"Live near to God, and so all things will appear to you little in comparison with eternal realities." - Robert Murray MCheyne

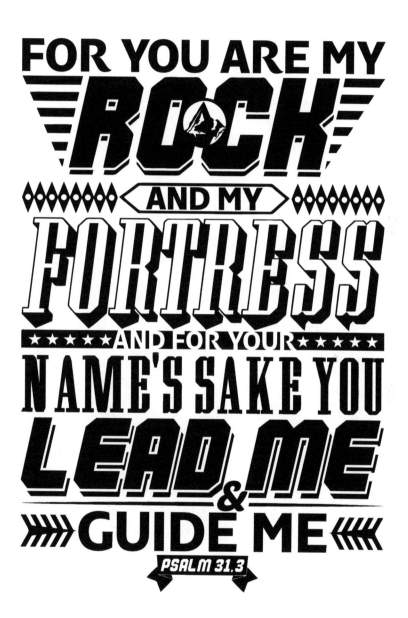

FOR YOU ARE MY ROCK AND MY FORTRESS AND FOR YOUR NAME'S SAKE YOU LEAD ME & GUIDE ME

PSALM 31.3

"The neglected heart will soon be a heart overrun with worldly thoughts; the neglected life will soon become a moral chaos; the church that is not jealously protected by mighty intercession and sacrificial labors will before long become the abode of every evil bird and the hiding place for unsuspected corruption. The creeping wilderness will soon take over that church that trusts in its own strength and forgets to watch and pray." - A. W. Tozer

"We have not been men of prayer. The spirit of prayer has slumbered among us. The closet has been too little frequented and delighted in. We have allowed business, study or active labor to interfere with our closet-hours. And the feverish atmosphere in which both the church and the nation are enveloped has found its way into our prayer closets." - Andrew Bonar

"Why is there so little forethought in the laying out of time and employment, so as secure a large portion of each day for prayer? Why is there so much speaking, yet so little prayer? Why Is there so much running to and fro to meetings, conventions, fellowship gatherings and yet so little time for prayer'? Brethren, why so many meetings with our fellow men and so few meetings with God?" - Andrew Bonar

"A godly man is a praying man. As soon as grace is poured in, prayer is poured out. Prayer is the soul's traffic with Heaven; God comes down to us by His Spirit, and we go up to Him by prayer." - Thomas Watson

"If I could hear Christ praying for me in the next room, I would not fear a million enemies. Yet distance makes no difference. He is praying for me." - Robert Murray M'Cheyne

"Men of prayer are men of faith; closet supplicants make faith's heroes." - The War Cry (1895)

"If I am concerned that my flock be men and women of prayer, then, as their pastor, I must lead the way; apathy in me will produce apathy in them. The church prayer meeting ought to be the best attended in the week, and if it is, success will follow the ministry of the Word at the weekends. I would rather a thousand times set men and women to pray than teach them to preach." " - J. D. Drysdale

"I would rather teach one man to pray than ten men to preach." - J. H. Jowett

"Oh, how few find time for prayer! There is time for everything else, time to sleep and time to eat, time to read the newspaper and the novel, time to visit friends, time for everything else under the sun, but-no time for prayer, the most important of all things, the one great essential!" -Oswald Smith

THE LIGHT

shines

IN THE **DARKNESS**

AND THE **DARKNESS**

has not

OVERCOME IT

JOHN 1.5

Date:

"On the mountains, torrents flow right along, cutting their own courses. But on the plains canals have to be dug out painfully by men so that the water might flow. So among those who live on the heights with God, the Holy Spirit makes its way through of its own accord, whereas those who devote little time to prayer and communion with God have to organize painfully." -Sadhu Sunder Singh

"Groanings which cannot be uttered are often prayers which cannot be refused." - C. H. Spurgeon

"God's greatest gifts to man come through travail. Whether we look into the spiritual or temporal sphere, can we discover anything, any great reform, any beneficial discovery, any soul-awakening revival, which did not come through the tolls and tears, the vigils and blood-shedding of men and woman whose sufferings were the pangs of Its birth?" - F. B. Meyer

"Some people become tired at the end of ten minutes or half an hour of prayer. What will they do when they have to spend Eternity in the presence of God? We must begin the habit here and become used to being with God." - Sadhu Sundar Singh

"Prayer is reaching out after the unseen; fasting is letting go of all that is seen and temporal. Fasting helps express, deepen, confirm the resolution that we are ready to sacrifice anything, even ourselves to attain what we seek for the kingdom of God." - Andrew Murray

"Continuing instant in prayer (Rom. 12:12). The Greek is a metaphor taken from hunting dogs that never give over the game till they have their prey." - Thomas Brooks

"If you are strangers to prayer you are strangers to power." - Billy Sunday

"Shall I give you yet another reason why you should pray? I have preached my very heart out. I could not say any more than I have said. Will not your prayers accomplish that which my preaching fails to do? Is it not likely that the Church has been putting forth its preaching hand but not its praying hand? Oh dear friends! Let us agonize in prayer." - C. H. Spurgeon

"A church in the land without the Spirit is rather a curse than a blessing. If you have not the Spirit of God, Christian worker, remember that you stand in somebody else's way; you are a fruitless tree standing where a fruitful tree might grow." - C. H. Spurgeon

Love

BELIEVES

all things

1 Cor. 13.7

"Pray, O pray, my brother! never, never quit your hold of the fullness of God; for time is nearly over, and if this fullness be lost it will be lost forever. I am astonished that we do not pray more, yea, that we do not live every moment as on the brink of the eternal world, and in the blessed expectation of that glorious country." - William Bramwell

"While women weep, as they do now, I'll fight; while children go hungry, as they do now I'll fight; while men go to prison, in and out, in and out, as they do now, I'll fight; while there is a drunkard left, while there is a poor lost girl upon the streets, while there remains one dark soul without the light of God, I'll fight - I'll fight to the very end!" - William Booth

"Work as if everything depended upon your work, and pray as if everything depended upon your prayer." - William Booth

"A real minister of the gospel is a man of prayer. Prayer is his grand employment, his safety, his first and perpetual duty; and under grace, the grand source of his consolation. Our instructions will be always barren, if they be not watered with our tears and prayers." - Thomas Coke

"A man may study because his brain is hungry for knowledge, even Bible knowledge. But he prays because his soul is hungry for God." - Leonard Ravenhill

"A minister, who prays not, who is not in love with prayer, is not a minister of the Church of God. He is a dry tree, which occupies in vain a place in Christ's garden. He is an enemy, and not a father, of the people. He is a stranger, who has taken the place of the shepherd, and to whom the salvation of the flock is an indifferent thing." - Thomas Coke

"In Shansi I found Chinese Christians who were accustomed to spend time in fasting and prayer. They recognized that this fasting, which so many dislike, which requires faith in God, since it makes one feel weak and poorly, is really a Divinely appointed means of grace. Perhaps the greatest hindrance to our work is our own imagined strength; and in fasting we learn what poor, weak creatures we are-dependent on a meal of meat for the little strength which we are so apt to lean upon." - J. Hudson Taylor

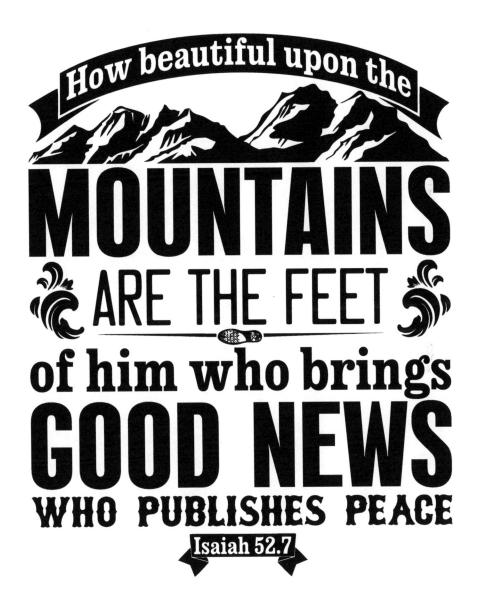

How beautiful upon the MOUNTAINS ARE THE FEET of him who brings GOOD NEWS WHO PUBLISHES PEACE

Isaiah 52.7

"Prayer is not designed to inform God, but to give man a sight of his misery; to humble his heart, to excite his desire, to inflame his faith, to animate his hope, to raise his soul from earth to heaven." - Adam Clarke

"They who pray not, know nothing of God, and know nothing of the state of their own souls." - Adam Clarke

"Let us advance upon our knees." - Joseph Neesima

"You must GO forward on your knees." - J. Hudson Taylor

"Satan does not care how many people read about prayer if only he can keep them from praying. When a church is truly convinced that prayer is where the action is, that church will so construct its corporate activities that the prayer program will have the highest priority." - Paul E. Billheimer

"Ministers who do not spend two hours a day in prayer are not worth a dime a dozen - degrees or no degrees." - Leonard Ravenhill

"The feeling of need and not the force of habit will make thee a sincere suppliant." - Evan Roberts

WAIT
for the
LORD
BE STRONG AND LET
Your
heart
take
COURAGE
wait for the LORD!
Psalm 27.14

"Prayer is buried, and lost and Heaven weeps. If all prayed the wicked would flee from our midst or to the refuge." - Evan Roberts

Date:

"Prayer is the midwife of mercy, that helps to bring it forth." - Matthew Henry

"You may as soon find a living man without breath as a living saint without prayer." - Matthew Henry

"The prayers and supplications that Christ offered up were, joined with strong cries and tears, herein setting us example not only to pray, but to be fervent and importunate in prayer. How many dry prayers, how few wet ones, do we offer up to God!" - Matthew Henry

"At God's counter there are no " SALE DAYS," for the price of revival is ever the same - TRAVAIL. - Leonard Ravenhill

"Workers that are strangers to knee work may work up a temporary excitement, but never will be able to secure the copious outpourings of genuine revival power." - Martin Wells Knapp

"It is in the field of prayer that life's critical battles are lost or won. We must conquer all our circumstances there. We must first of all bring them there. We must survey them there. We must master them there. In prayer we bring our spiritual enemies into the Presence of God and we fight them there. Have you tried that? Or have you been satisfied to meet and fight your foes in the open spaces of the world?" - J. H. Jowett

The grass withers
the flower fades
but the
WORD
of our
GOD
will stand
FOREVER
Isaiah 40.8

"He that leaves off prayer leaves off the fear of God. You cast off fear, and restrain prayer before God (Job 15: 4). A man that leaves off prayer is capable of any wickedness. When Saul had given up inquiring of God he went to the witch of Endor"
- Thomas Watson

The angel fetched Peter out of prison, but it was prayer that fetched the angel."-
Thomas Watson

"Prayer will make a man cease from sin, or sin will entice a man to cease from prayer." - John Bunyan

"We know the utility of prayer from the efforts of the wicked spirits to distract us during the divine office; and we experience the fruit of prayer in the defeat of our enemies."- John Climacus

"Pray often; for prayer is a shield to the soul, a sacrifice to God, and a scourge for Satan." - John Bunyan

"No one is a firmer believer in the power of prayer than the devil; not that he practices it, but he suffers from it." -Guy H. King

"When we go to God by prayer, the devil knows we go to fetch strength against him, and therefore he opposeth us all he can." - Richard Sibbes

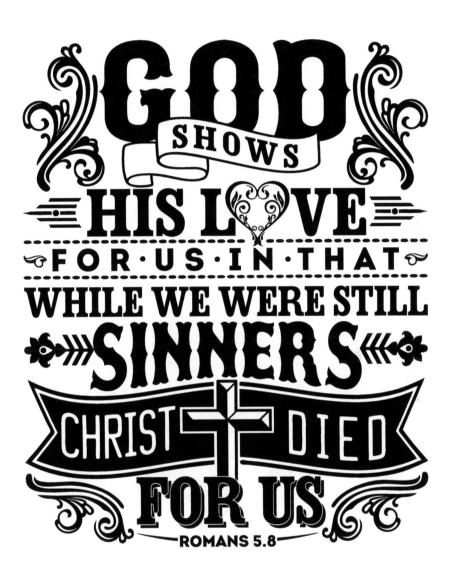

"Christ was in an agony at prayer (Luke 22: 44). Many when they pray are rather in a lethargy, than in an agony. When they are about the world they are all fire; when they are at prayer, they are all Ice." - Thomas Watson

"If I cannot hear 'the sound of rain' long before the rain falls, and then go out to some hilltop of the Spirit, as near to my God as I can and have faith to wait there with my face between my knees, though six times or sixty times I am told 'there is nothing', till at last there arises a little cloud out of the sea, then I know nothing of Calvary love." (Read 1 Kings 18:41-45). - Amy Carmichael

"It will not do for us to go to Heaven by ourselves. We must be on fire, friends for saving others. To be workers will draw heaven down and will draw others to heaven . Without a readiness to work, the Spirit of prayer will not come." - Evan Roberts

"Prayer is the secret of power." - Evan Roberts

"Secret prayer is the spring-time of life." - Evan Roberts

"A man who is intimate with God will never be intimidated by men." - Leonard
Ravenhill

"It will never be altogether well with us till we convert the universe into a prayer room, and continue in the Spirit as we go from place to place.... The prayer hour is left standing before God till the other hours come and stand beside it; then, if they are found to be a harmonious sisterhood, the prayer is granted." - George Bowen

This is the
DAY
THAT THE
LORD
HAS MADE
let us
REJOICE
AND BE GLAD IN IT
Psalm 118.24

"The main lesson about prayer is just this: Do it! Do it! Do it! You want to be taught to pray. My answer is pray and never faint, and then you shall never fail. There is no peradventure. You cannot fail.... A sense of real want is at the very root of prayer." - John Laidlaw

"Prayer is the means by which we obtain all the graces that rain down upon us from the divine Fountain of Goodness and Love." - Laurence Scupoli

"None can believe how powerful prayer is, and what it is able to effect, but those who have learned it by experience. It is a great matter when in extreme need to take hold on prayer. I know whenever I have prayed earnestly that I have been amply heard, and have obtained more than I prayed for. God indeed sometimes delayed, but at last He came." - Martin Luther

"It has often been said that prayer is the greatest force in the universe. This is no exaggeration. It will bear constant repetition. In this atomic age when forces are being released that stagger the thought and imagination of man, it is well to remember that prayer transcends all other forces." - F. J. Huegel

"If the church would only awaken to her responsibility of intercession, we could well evangelize the world in a short time. It is not God's plan that the world be merely evangelized ultimately. It should be evangelized in every generation. There should be a constant gospel witness in every corner of the world so that no sinner need close his eyes in death without hearing the gospel, the good news of salvation through Christ." - T. A. Hegre

"Hell is larger today than it was yesterday, because many of us have failed to pray." -
David Smithers

"There is no power like that of prevailing prayer, of Abraham pleading for Sodom, Jacob wrestling in the stillness of the night, Moses standing in the breach, Hannah intoxicated with sorrow, David heartbroken with remorse and grief, Jesus in sweat of blood. Add to this list from the records of the church your personal observation and experience, and always there is the cost of passion unto blood. Such prayer prevails. It turns ordinary mortals into men of power. It brings power. It brings fire. It brings rain. It brings life. It brings God." - Samuel Chadwick

We love
because
He first
loved
us

1 John 4.19

"To strive in prayer means to struggle through those hindrances which would restrain or even prevent us entirely from continuing in persevering prayer. It means to be so watchful at all times that we can notice when we become slothful in prayer and that we go to the Spirit of prayer to have this remedied. In this struggle, too, the decisive factor is the Spirit of prayer." - O. Hallesby

"Once a poor soul entered the school of prayer after his arrival in hell. He asked for relief from his agony; it was refused. He asked that a beggar warn his brothers; he was turned down. He was praying to Abraham, a man; he could not locate God. He dared not ask to get out; he plainly knew that he was beyond all hope. Prayerless on earth, unanswered in hell, he suffers on as the man who tried to learn to pray too late." - Cameron V. Thompson

"Of all the duties enjoined by Christianity none is more essential and yet more neglected than prayer. Most people consider the exercise a fatiguing ceremony, which they are justified in abridging as much as possible. Even those whose profession or fears lead them to pray, pray with such languor and wanderings of mind that their prayers, far from drawing down blessings, only increase their condemnation." - Fenelon

"How hard is it sometimes to get leave of hearts to seek God! Jesus Christ went more willingly to the cross than we do to the throne of grace." - Thomas Watson "The Western church has lost the prayer stamina of the mission churches in Asia, Africa, South America, Indonesia, and those of the underground church in many parts of the world. Yes, we are great organizers, but poor pray-ers." - Paul E. Billheimer

"The prayer of faith is the only power in the universe to which the great Jehovah yields. Prayer is the sovereign remedy." - Robert Hall

"The men who have done the most for God in this world have been early on their knees. He who fritters away the early morning, its opportunity and freshness, in other pursuits than seeking God will make poor headway seeking Him the rest of the day. If God is not first in our thoughts and efforts in the morning, He will be in the last place the remainder of the day." - E. M. Bounds

"Oh brother, pray; in spite of Satan, pray; spend hours in prayer; rather neglect friends than not pray; rather fast, and lose breakfast, dinner, tea, and supper - and sleep too - than not pray. And we must not talk about prayer, we must pray in right earnest. The Lord is near. He comes softly while the virgins slumber." - Andrew A. Bonar

FEAR NOT

STAND FIRM

& SEE

the SALVATION

of the LORD

WHICH HE WILL

WORK FOR YOU

TODAY

EXODUS 14.13

Whole days and WEEKS have I spent prostrate on the ground in silent or vocal prayer." - George Whitefteld

"All decays begin in the closet; no heart thrives with out much secret converse with God, and nothing will make amends for the want of it." - John Berridge "A man can not lead others where he is not willing to go himself. Therefore, beware of the prayerless church leader who no longer readily admits his own need for more of the person and power of Jesus Christ. Only a seeking, praying heart can truly encourage spiritual HUNGER in others!" Ð David Smithers

"God never intended His Church to be a refrigerator in which to preserve perishable piety. He intended it to be an incubator in which to hatch out converts." - F. Lincicome

"There can be no revival when Mr. Amen and Mr. Wet-Eyes are not found in the audience." - Charles G. Finney

"Let me burn out for God. After all, whatever God may appoint, prayer is the great thing. Oh, that I may be a man of prayer!" - Henry Martyn

"Love is kindled in a flame, and ardency is its life. Flame is the air which true Christian experience breathes. It feeds on fire; it can withstand anything rather than a feeble flame; but when the surrounding atmosphere is frigid or lukewarm, it dies, chilled and starved to its vitals. True prayer MUST be aflame." - E. M. Bounds

Date:

"God's cause is committed to men; God commits Himself to men. Praying men are the vice-regents of God; they do His work and carry out His plans." - E. M. Bounds

HE HEALS the BROKENHEARTED and BINDS UP their WOUNDS
—Psalm 147.3

"Prayer is the acid test of devotion." - Samuel Chadwick

"All the resources of the Godhead are at our disposal!" - Jonathan Goforth

"Prayer and Pains, through faith in Jesus Christ will do anything." - John Elliot

"God loves with a great love the man whose heart is bursting with a passion for the IMPOSSIBLE." - William Booth

"I have found that there are three stages in every great work of God: first, it is impossible, then it is difficult, then it is done." ~ Hudson Taylor

"Faith sees the invisible, believes the unbelievable, and receives the impossible."-
Corrie ten Boom

"We never test the resources of God until we attempt the IMPOSSIBLE." - F. B. Meyer

LOVE

does not rejoice at wrongdoing

BUT REJOICES
WITH THE TRUTH 1COR. 13.6

"Until we reach for the IMPOSSIBLE through fervent, faith-filled prayer, we will NEVER fulfill our created purpose!" - David Smithers

"A church without an intelligent, well-organized, and systematic prayer program is simply operating a religious treadmill." - Paul E. Billheimer

"God will do nothing but in answer to prayer." - John Wesley

"The greatest thing anyone can do for God and for man is to pray. You can do more than pray after you have prayed, but you cannot do more than pray until you have prayed. Prayer is striking the winning blow ... service is gathering up the results." - S. D. Gordon

"Don't pray when you feel like it. Have an appointment with the Lord and keep it. A man is powerful on his knees." - Corrie ten Boom

"Is prayer your steering wheel or your spare tire?" - Corrie ten Boom

"Jesus Christ carries on intercession for us in heaven; the Holy Ghost carries on intercession in us on earth; and we the saints have to carry on intercession for all men." - Oswald Chambers

JESUS SAID
come
UNTO ME
I WILL GIVE YOU
rest

Matthew 11.28

"Our prayers lay the track down which God's power can come. Like a mighty locomotive, his power is irresistible, but it cannot reach us without rails." - Watchman Nee

"Pray not for crutches but for wings." - Phillips Brooks

"Prayer does not enable us to do a greater work for God. Prayer is a greater work for God." - Thomas Chalmers

"Prayer is not learned in a classroom but in the closet." - E. M. Bounds

"Prayer is not monologue, but dialogue. God's voice in response to mine is its most essential part." - Andrew Murray

"Prayer is weakness leaning on omnipotence." - W. S. Bowden

"Prayerlessness is a sin." - Corrie ten Boom

IF GOD IS FOR US WHO CAN BE AGAINST US?

ROMANS 8.31

"Satan trembles when he sees the weakest saint upon his knees." - William Cowper

"Some men will spin out a long prayer telling God who and what he is, or they pray out a whole system of divinity. Some people preach, others exhort the people, till everybody wishes they would stop, and God wishes so, too, most undoubtedly." - Charles G. Finney

"Some people think God does not like to be troubled with our constant coming and asking. The way to trouble God is not to come at all." - D. L. Moody "Prayerlessness is a sin." - Corrie ten Boom

Date:

"Satan trembles when he sees the weakest saint upon his knees." - William Cowper

"Some men will spin out a long prayer telling God who and what he is, or they pray out a whole system of divinity. Some people preach, others exhort the people, till everybody wishes they would stop, and God wishes so, too, most undoubtedly." - Charles G. Finney

"Some people think God does not like to be troubled with our constant coming and asking. The way to trouble God is not to come at all." - D. L. Moody

"Talking to men for God is a great thing, but talking to God for men is greater still." -
E. M. Bounds

My SOUL thirsts... for the living GOD

Psalm 42.2

"The Christian on his knees sees more than the philosopher on tiptoe." - D. L. Moody

"The one concern of the devil is to keep Christians from praying. He fears nothing from prayerless studies, prayerless work, and prayerless religion. He laughs at our toil, mocks at our wisdom, but trembles when we pray." - Samuel Chadwick

"There is nothing that makes us love a man so much as praying for him." - William Law

"We are too busy to pray, and so we are too busy to have power. We have a great deal of activity, but we accomplish little; many services but few conversions; much machinery but few results." - R. A. Torrey

"You shall find this to be God's usual course: not to give his children the taste of his delights till they begin to sweat in seeking after them." - Richard Baxter

Made in the USA
Lexington, KY
18 November 2018